Double Agent

2011 Winner of the Kore Press First Book Award selected by Bhanu Kapil

Double Agent

poems

MICHELLE CHAN BROWN

KORE PRESS + TUCSON + 2012

standing by women's words since 1993

Kore Press, Inc., Tucson, Arizona USA
www.korepress.org

Designed by Sally Geier
Cover photo by Larry Hammerness
Set in Beton and Bell Centennial
Printed in the United States of America.

We express our gratitude to those who make Kore Press publications possible: individuals,
the Tucson-Pima Arts Council, the Arizona Commission on the Arts, through appropriations
from the Arizona State Legislature and the National Endowment for the Arts.

ISBN 978-1-888553-52-9

Library of Congress Cataloging-in-Publication Data

Brown, Michelle Chan, 1981-
Double agent : poems / Michelle Chan Brown.
     p. cm.
I. Title.
PS3602.R72235D68 2012
811'.6--dc22
                              2012020904

For Paul

CONTENTS

III

We follow blindly, clad in coats of pink,
A beast whose nature is to run and stink.
I am civilized in my pink but
Civilized is about having stuff.

— FREDERICK SEIDEL, "KILL POEM"

We came down from the north
Blue hands and a torch
Red wine and food for free
A possibility
We share our mothers' health
Is that what we've been dealt
What's in it for me?
Fine
Then I'll agree

— THE KNIFE, "WE SHARE OUR MOTHERS' HEALTH"

I

DOUBLE AGENT

There was cake & honey
wine at the naturalization ceremony,

friends dressed up like old lovers.
There was money, the Victrola,

the old patriotic songs. Everyone drunk
on peanuts, nostalgia just-so sweet.

The sign above the antique garrotte:
No running allowed, please.

We passed modified foods.
Our talk was small enough for the laden table.

They cut the ribbon. At the bar's end,
I scrubbed my face off.

I pledged — well, allegiance.
I stuck my false leg out.

This was the opening move,
love's schlocky minuet.

Handsome drone, you seemed
numerous in the mirrored room.

You tripped, saluted with firepower.
You stuttered: live wire, no fault.

I widened my paste eyes, flashed my jewelry.
I salivated and rubbed my yellow like a moon.

It's always going to be November, isn't it?
They'll drive back the rain

with their black gloves & clear umbrellas,
their equal-opportunity grins.

Emboldened by my regional costume,
I attempted the mother tongue.

Nice earpiece, I said, by way of introduction.
It's our *language now,* you said.

BLIND DATE WITH MY FATHER, 1976

If you squint or lose a contact, he could almost be Pushkin
with a spray-tan. Right off, he orders sherry, confesses
that he spends too much time with cooking shows,
smooth jazz on public radio. The Cold War is on.
Everyone's mad for beets & boycotting bluejeans.
In the restaurant's bathroom, I rub off my lipstick,
strive for Eastern Bloc chic, but my father can't stop
scribbling on napkins, that crucial last chapter on the lives
of minor noblemen. *That's fascinating,* I whisper, all that incest
and quashing of rebellion. His mouth's too full of mussels
to reply. I dip my pinkie in the lemon butter, poke our initials
in the salmon paté. All of this is being captured on camera,
but my skirt has a mind of its own. He tries to play-fight
with the copper candelabra, tells me he's looking
for *something, you know, long-term.* The wineglasses
are listening. The breadbasket's gone to sleep. I've polished
my good boots for this, with cognac spittle and tears,
dusted my décolletage with the ash of cigarillo, but I can't
eat a thing when the sommelier circles like the avenging
vulture of nightcaps & the horoscopes pair me with Nikita
Khrushchev or the ugly member of the Bee Gees, & my father
is dousing his sickle-print tie in the horseradish vodka
as the matchboxes cackle & it's surely not his first time
at this but nonetheless he doesn't offer to pick up the check.

BAIT

They're dragging the Volga for bodies again.
Still the men fish.

My father says:
I wouldn't eat anything that came out of here.

The fishermen spit into their beer.
I am a girlish shard

in their amber bottles, but
they are hardly grandfatherly.

My father says:
I wouldn't kill anything I couldn't eat.

Impossible to decipher the headlines,
the policemen with tender

collarbones under blue.
He's got an eye on you.

His glossy baton flirts with the edge
of my skirt. He says: *Papers.*

OPEN HOUSE

Step inside, there's Beluga! A round of earpieces for everyone. A round of children. If
we run out of anything, there's the host, filling every corner, neutral as flour. If your exit
strategies aren't met, observe the fleet of Arabian horses kitty-corner to
the hearses.

The guests stamp and sniff. They are pillars of society. Hence the faces of stone. They
do not concern themselves with the ethics of eating endangered species. 1984 is an era
of optimism, after all: we've kept our assets at arms' length. We've bobbed out the bad
apples.

Mother is frantic with the ashtray, collecting like an archaeologist's assistant. Her black
taffeta's cut on the bias. We live in the eighth Stalin sister. Father, the aesthete, displays a
hunk of Berlin Wall in our curio cabinet. Grumpy Brezhnev mugs on our drink coasters.

Insemination occurs by canapé. Thirteen tulips heighten the bouquet's tension. Bouf-
fants float in the atmosphere like funereal chrysanthemums. Bosoms swing low. Ears
jockey. Pomade is positively incendiary. *Excuse me, sir, your anecdote's
showing.*

All the women siphon monogrammed napkins & keys & Valium & Tsar Nicolai from
our kitchen cabinet, kiss me like a sister. *Your father has the soul of a boyar,* they say.
Don't shoot the messenger! is Father's favorite toast. The G-men secure real Lugers in
the cheeks of their gabardine.

Nothing's ready, Mother hisses. We're all suspicious of the *bon mot.* She squares her
shoulder pads. She's gaunt from so much merrymaking, so many changes of clothes.
In the night's deep, my mother riffles through the photos, latex gloves bloody with
Maraschinos.

ENEMY

Genial. Harmless as a new hat.
That is the way of plagues.

The father said: *What smells so good?*
The mother said: *Nothing ventured.*

Nothing demanded. Nothing fed
Or cooked. The plague was modest,

Refusing the royal "we"—
The plague dispelled myths

Like candy shell. Not metaphor,
But meat and bone. Not religion,

But man. Lo, the plague was traditional.
Notes the anthropologist: *Traditions kill.*

He held the baby on his knee. He built
The built-in bookshelf. By god, he was lively.

First, the flora fell. Later the animals.
Grief came organic to the children.

The girl wrote: *Only the dog is noble.*
They'll eat off the family tree.

History told them: no one ever starved
For love. The mother darned

Old flags for their cadavers.
After a time, they grew accustomed

To the maggots' fancy footwork.
Each had been told: *you carry the world.*

Their shoulders were thin as saplings.
The children stroked the sofa's stems.

Laughter filled their backpacks.
It is always almost the same.

COMPOUND

We are building a maze for all the rabbits that have infested the compound. The school-children are terrified, throwing their colorful backpacks in the river, hiding their lunch-meat in their mouths. What's on everyone's lips is *sugar, sugar, sugar.* These rabbits are big-eyed and solicitous; they eschew human clothing but are enthusiasts of the cosmetic. I eye them outside my window, the sensuous arc of their haunches, the scattershot of their hind paws. So robustly athletic. They hear something, they do, with those milky ears. They hear our plans for renovation, the brick-and-mortar construction of our fears.

Psychics claim the consul had a pet rabbit that she loved too little. The corpse is unsettling the river reeds by the old canning factory. The psychiatrists can't deny our over-identification with the vermin population; they remind us how close we are to being near misses. My father turns down the sheets and tells me I'm funnier than the prettiest bunny you'll ever meet.

I stir the stew for hours. I add rosemary, chicory, carrot, coriander, hearts of palm. I add placenta, newspaper, causes for alarm. I take the vintage carcass (1981) and slit him whisker to stomach. Cinnamon, five-spice, horsehair, liquor. The ice crystals titter on the white countertop, and as my belly-full love sleeps, the rabbit army feasts on his delicacies. He snores *sugar, sugar, sugar.*

AUTOBIOGRAPHY

Inside, beside the habitual
pickles, cream, caffeine, bland gold band,
prenatal vitamins big as quartz & mercury,
I slept the sleep of a bell.
So clear. So sweet. So the question goes:
A bird or a plane? A bottle or a man?
In the city around her, rockets tested the sky.
The windmills hummed their song
through the nuclear plants: *A time, a time*
for kindling. She was stink and flesh, carcinogens.
She grabbed her shovel, hiked up her housedress.
In the luminous yard, she buried her pearls
& her placenta. She lined her hopes,
those bright jelly-bellies, all along the bassinette.

SECOND-IN-COMMAND

And on his granite mantle, the season's pests:
pelts striped eclectic by a callousness

of barbed wire. And on his stereo,
the chirps of the concrete jungle.

And on his gun rack? Guns.
The house plants, furious with oxygen,

and the fruit—
venal. No fear of hybrids here.

The pears, the plums, the cross-eyed cherries.
He took the ugly with the pure.

Unstrung, the beaks of the overtalkers.
Their class rings and honorifics

screamed electric in his custom flue.
I thought, *trophies, really?*

I was gunning to outgrow such boots.
By way of explanation, he said "Trophies.

Really." With care, he assessed my appetites;
with canny sincerity, the Lurex thread

of my commitment. I swear, I was full
of easy living, listening evenly

to the wistful dissidents. I was up
to the gum in sugar, in worms,

blunting my teeth on spoils.
Reader, I swear—

A weak man cannot make exceptions,
he said. To be mercenary is a crime

against womanhood. So I sipped vintages
of the river, where father and I

once caught salmon.
I breathed out as they breathed death in.

Reader, do consider
the consequences of overbreeding.

O river. O villages in abandon.
Of course, one must make exceptions, he said.

I threw the littlest fish to the rocky shore.
Reader, I swear I loved him.

KUNSTKAMERA

Maybe I should have skipped
breakfast. The line's
longer than ever,
circling the building
like a stethoscope.
Docile in their summer
best, babies spit up
shawls of crystal
on their mothers,
fathers flash pectorals
under mesh tank tops.
I can't tell if their hands
are poised for clapping
or down their pants.
This crowd has come
prepared, their meals in
plastic bags emblazoned
with snapshots of the marginally
famous. They're concealing
whole lemons, pellets
of bread, sweating vodka.
Slivers of salami
like an amputated arm—
striation, muscle, ivory fat.
Someone's taking a picture,
bullet-fast, and I know
I'm in it, pretty in slingbacks
and a surgical mask.
In my purse, a notebook
safe as forceps, a baggie
of unshelled peanuts.
The guards sweat
in bowties and rubber spats.
Our money is good enough
to melt here, so humid;

our game faces pool
on the marble. First floor:
ears in brine, two fetuses
fused at the skull. The show
has already started. The tourists
adjust their glasses.

PINS & NEEDLES

My mother's back bent like a question
mark. I knew the work of her, the fix

& fuss & cover, better than my own name.
Nerves sheathed our tablecloth and lined

our mattress. *For God's sake,* my father said,
do something useful. Afraid of her teeth,

the implied threat of their stance,
she sanctioned necessities: her smile,

her feedings. *For God's sake,* my father said.
we're in public. The live-in servants pinched

thread for ceremonial shrouds.
The city, alas, was burning, along

with the butcher's best pork.
No one to amend this. My sister

stretched her brassiere collection
across the neighborhood, a one-girl

vaudeville of gore and Jean Naté.
Her indigent audience slinked in

and out, all hours. I wrote: *Someday
I will know what is important.*

The neighborhood brightened with bombs.
For God's sake, said my father, *not in the house.*

The telephone jangled, mad as a Kewpie.
We were always being called

to headquarters. We expected miracles
from our bodies. I wrote: *Thin tastes better*

than any food. There was no end to propaganda.
I was searching for the right word,

incorrectly. A silver spoon blackened
my black tongue. And my mother, slurring

at the dictionary—couldn't she tell
error from *arrow?* ENGLISH ONLY

read the signs at the embassy. Door-to-
door, I sold knives to the wives of consuls.

I bequeathed cherry bombs to their kids'
tree houses. Said the servants:

These are grave times. I hold them close as love.
I want to sink into the backs of true

men, the generals and electricians,
the talkers and takers of might.

I'll live on plumes and wiring.
My mother was afraid of her fingers.

She squirreled them in the dry crevices
of the furniture. *Desiccate there, little liars,*

she'd croon, rocking herself into her fear
in her genuine rocking chair.

MEMORANDUM

Unease, green scheme of, runs deep
in the city's bowels, purifies what we think.
Consider life as a scherzo. Throw that out.
We wear our American luck like a fannypack.
The pretender queen has lost her marbles.
She tears up flowers. She counts the petals.
She loses count. The natives have absconded
with the hardware and the silk. Please send
a man who fixes things. Please send towels.
These curtains are pretty and incompetent.
They can't brush off the shouting in the streets.
Our recommendations were soft as cashmere.
We wrote it, loud and clear. *Don't visit.*
Didn't you hear us? *Come quickly. Bring power.*

COLONY OF THE NEW TEMPERANCE

If we shed our faces at the entry —
        what were they to us? We were seized
           by relief, who wore a uniform

of false feathers. Still, we dreamers gripped our unease.
        In the floral gloom, cask and casket looked the same.
           Just drink what's given, said the walls.

So we did. Thus had our fathers survived; our mothers,
        by painting silence into the wallpaper's trim.
           The blue fumes of the old houses!

The family portraits, dimmed by the bottle's superb algae.
        We could cork up what stank.
           Just live in the present, said the walls,

and we conceded to the décor's odd power.
        We dismissed sensation like the snowflakes
           above our parents' picnics. Like fingerprints.

Our fathers stood at the wells, scooped water with their hands.
        Our mothers pushed in cotton,
           soaked up all there was inside them.

AUTOBIOGRAPHY (II)

My mother said: *Please no one except the enemy.*
Listen. Take your hat off.

Your bracelets. Your spectacles, your smell of exits.

     The coat with the military buttons.
The cheongsam, the cashmere cardigan, the burqua,
    the lipstick (China Red) the ash blond hairpiece dubbed *money—*

            into the drawer.
                It's warm here,

        by the fire, and my fingers are dirtied from the ashes.
     Please clean them.
The dishes loll over the sink. They're ready to crack. Please solder them.

          The drowsing jade plants. Please water them.

That bag of old tricks, wearing my black hair,
     my strawberry birthmark, my yellow bodysuit:
       Please set her on fire.

          Fire!

Gather me up
  in your arms and water me until I'm wearing the slicker over nothing.

I'm wearing cleavage.
My promises drip down my haunches,
sludge & tallow.   Yes, yellow

Reads *crafty,* means *fear.*

      My mother said: *Believe in what you do not see.*

PLEASURING THE ENEMY

If you don't like eating we can go to the movies.
If you don't like movies we can go the opera.

The symphony. Let's moon over the cellist.
The protest. Let's chant our own names,

join the cult and forego our worldly goods,
release our balloons into the sorghum ether,

play chemistry or make caramel in the kitchen,
wear orange and go hunt the last town over.

Or you can wear orange and I'll shave my head
so my ears lie flat as an animal's. You can hunt me,

and when I'm shivved to pieces on your pokers,
you can hold me over the campfire and nudge

marrons glacés into my nostrils. You can stuff me
and sit me by the fire with a round of Chinese checkers.

I'll let you win. I'll let you keep me in the closet,
teetering on high boots, dirty-talking the hangers.

You give a leather mask a real personality. I feel
the edge of every bad-sex dream

knifing its merry way under my eyelids.
My medicine cabinet topples from the heft

of your medicine, and my walls soften like crêpe
from your heavy breath. I'm that mess.

I'm in the dustbin—make me pretty,
or at least clean. Or at least dirty. I want

to know the soul. I want to be free of the body,
the legs that spread easy as chopsticks.

It's warm where you are. Someone's crying
in the other room. Give me the chatty skeleton I can live in.

II

THE TITLE "LOVE POEM" ALREADY EXISTS

I'm terrified. Can I say that?
I bit your cheek off as a defense
mechanism, & it's a lie
to declare it's more than I can
chew. My greed bores
me & a few & now you're sleeping—
the cognac is warm & the mating
cicadas are restless or maybe committing
mass suicide outside our window
but I'm off track because you're naked
& long & lovely, blanching sheets
I haven't cleaned since I was born.
There's a jar of paste in the fridge
that I eat standing up & lonesome.
I want to jut my tongue through
your aquiline nose into the seething
sediment of your brain matter, soft
palate, nip the weathered jelly
of your fingers. See, they've been touching
someone else & I can't bear it. My jealousy
is the veneered shelf where I keep
all the sentimental novels
I'm ashamed of. I've been bleeding
fountain pen all over you,
drafting tattoos of sad cuts
of meat to adorn your shoulders.
Can I say I'd like to sit on them—
ride you, be small enough
to fit in a sling across your dangerous
belly, die early & be reborn, swing
on the highest branches until I'm shrieking,
fake ambitious jumps and deliver
nothing but what I've promised, so as
to break beautifully in the yawning
sand below, so as to scoop & carve you up,
make you liquid, drink you?

SHIPWRECK

What we heard about thirst was true.
Everywhere, water. Everywhere, salt.
And we drank it. We learned to love
our crumpling bones. Each sunspot
on our skin deserved a christening.
Distance gifted the world a shimmer.
Time passed, perhaps. We grew wolfish.
Spears of birdcall. Unthinkable birds.
We searched for the isle of women.
We searched for our dead fathers.
We searched for the hardware store.
We were used to solitude. Some of us
had worked the mills, where skylights cracked
and loaned us stars. We learned to relish
the ownership of hours. Our sheets
acceded to the torpor. If you must,
call it sickness— the sea colonized us.
Below muslin, our heartbeats thrilled,
lazy as laps. Breezes licked our faces flat.
If we wept, we wept soundless as sand.
What wave would betray our trust?

THE RETIREMENT HOME FOR NUNS

A sink in every room & on the wall,
the bare white outlines of the crucifix, spindly

as a girl's shoulder, a saint's clavicle.
The pause before an answer.

They threw themselves from the garrets.
When we make love on our altar

of empty bottles, you weigh the benefits
of the monastery. Get thee

between my thighs, or I'll take
the company of a handsomer beast.

At night, the cat stalks their ghosts
& I walk unevenly around the edge

of their drowning pool. Word was
they wore roller skates

under their habits, catcalled the moon.
Living alone with a seeing-eye

portrait (Mary) one develops
certain habits, e.g. a permanent

lipstick print on the chalice
of cut-rate port. What did those sisters

hide under their wimples: a thousand
solutions to the crossword puzzle,

pornography, a discourse
on the sainthood? *Wimple*

is so close to *whimper.* In the bed
where Mother Superior must

have heaved her spindled bones,
you crouch quiet as a gargoyle.

The sun etches the tombstones
in the yard. What does stone scare

away—intruders, harbingers of the devil,
the one I've been waiting for?

Yesterday she knocked three times
on my door, whispered *here,*

here is where I used to worship, hung
her body reverent as rosary beads

over the waxed floor. She spread
her hands toward me, as though

I could shrink myself into her skin,
or grow the length of a harmless serpent,

coil her holy blood into a vise.
The end is near, I said, to break the ice.

HYPNOSIS

The stage smells of grape bubblegum & vomit & Love's
Baby Soft, but the man's mustache, oily as mink, bobs up,
steady as a white boy's back. *Sleep, sleep, dance.* He laughs.
He's full of spells and we love him. We cup
each other, bend forward, use our ponytails as whips.
All the Lizzies, MaryJos & Karens are going crazy—
their pupils darken, their row of eyes a uniform ellipsis.
Their little feet can't touch the floor. You see,
he makes it look so easy. The frail girls holler
but we can't hear them over the persistent scrim
of music, beautiful as dragonflies soldered
to a Mason jar. Our mothers said beware of him
with black boots, a cowlick and a pretty, pretty ring.
When we wake up, we'll remember everything.

APOLLO 11

I.

All the July nights, they sleep close enough for nothing to burrow between. But it does. Specks, freckles, spackle. Dermis or dirt. Under the carpet, in the red nectarine flesh, in the walls & the ceiling. Between the slab of her thigh and the scythe of his upper arm. In the telephone wiring. They'll be fingered. They toss and moan, scratch themselves raw. They babble in Morse. They start awake. Who's listening?

II.

The act of contact equals the act of butchery. His belly is long and translucent, a sheet of glass. When they touch in dreams, she can make out what he consumes. All the curious jellyfish. The mud castles of boyhood. His innards are a museum display. The eager nubs of her fingers made her an art thief, clumsy. She wants & wants. She regrets she cannot attend the auction.

III.

They lie naked. The moon landing is broadcast on television. The bugs flatten on them. They are wondrous as cars. They honeymoon. They Getaway. They bring lubricants to the motor inn. A single tube of toothpaste. Two blood tests; two certificates of birth. From the televisions of other rooms, other 'mooners, they hear a chorus. One small step for mankind. She says *Let's try once more.*

IV.

July nights bleed into cool July mornings. July mornings smother afternoons, red as embryo. The minutes tramp on, relentless. Are they losing the race? Hearts and minds, economics. Gas mask of sunscreen, egg yolk sky. She cannot stand this heat but her heart belongs in the kitchen. Pool-madness spreads thickly over the subdivisions and neighborhoods and towns. An infestation, a sickness.

V.

Someone's always following me, she says. *I'm afraid. They keep adding lanes to the highway. Stations to the radio. Shelters below the houses. And they're always changing hats, and the paint of their cars. They think they can get away with it.* He says: *You have to bury it.* She says: *Yesterday, after the doctors', I parked on the shoulder. Our meat turned. I could smell it. And the heat burned through my skirt.* He kisses her belly, her face. *I'm expecting an important phone call. Is supper ready? Whenever you feel up to it,* he says. *No hurry.*

VI.

The pools & then the televisions. The wives' beehives nearly to the ceiling. *Dear big new house, please carry me away. I will build you higher and higher if that means I can access heaven.* It's November. Wives rise en masse from their ultrasuede sofas. Ants bear 50 times their body weight. A marvel, no? The black legs uncomplaining under ears of corn. The ants march. The troops march. The villagers march. The Reds march. The wives march. Television trays are a colorful, fragile armor.

VII.

The moon-men, too, take part in the march. Their white suits are the uniforms of exterminators. *Know thy enemy,* they were told. They people the lunar surface like stitches to an ivory bias-cut dress. They listen for the alien murmurings. They forgot the translator. But they beautify nothing; there is no endpoint, no party. The moon is a carcass gnawed clean. They finger her craters over and over, heedless as graffiti artists. They right flags disinterestedly to prove the mission.

SAVE THE FACE

For the educated, a minor challenge—
like birding, breeding, or archery.

No point in seeing
the blown-up body.

Our mouths can move
with the usual vivid things.

Nights, though, we wake up to the smell
lifting the white collars of our gowns.

We vow to get out more,
but we've had our fill

of scenery, chopped down the apple tree,
the phone lines, the daffodils.

The little corpses of our souls!
They're smiling up at our stethoscopes.

We carry nothing but scalpels.
Terror keeps us sharp; it's no miracle

of modern science,
my face on hers.

It's a paper bag with holes for eyes, a shadow
gash for a mouth.

In the business,
we say *beyond recognition*.

OF THE MOTHERLAND

He sniffs her coccyx, a mango from the black market.
Ashgabat is lovely at this time of year.
Summer bleeds the rats onto the pavement (wretched)
but their whirled fur makes a carpet we can clear
in flying leaps, or high-heeled goose steps. Here, *then*
comes before *if*. The beds make us pale or bloodless:
nothing will hide in them, save for the stems
we plucked those wild nights in the communal forest,
in government-sanctioned domiciles. Take a nap
in wedding cakes, ignored by the dictator, who writes
slapstick autobiographies on the bodies of his wives.
He licks her backbone's crucifix. Who lied re: the lack of maps— ?

AUTOBIOGRAPHY (III)

The oracle said:
>   *He will come to you on a black horse.*
>   I snort.
>   Who rides horses anymore?

                              *

I want a Lamborghini, a wheezing Fiat.
        I'll settle for a Teflon-plated minivan. Just a vehicle:

four walls and working door   a tricky lock   just a safe place to die
                                                    just a way

to see real cities,
the kick & wit of dust in the backcountry.

We'll do the donut holes in the financial district
and we'll rob banks, too, amuse the cold moon
                                    and throw out lovers

like a youthful treatise.   We don't need rules, my king,

we just need more discipline   willpower   money.

                            So you take a little extra.

That's OK. You are the responsible party
            I don't even have
my license, only a half-full suitcase and a pashmina

                            to strangle down what I don't really mean.

Those wrecked street signs sure look wrecked.

        Surely the crowds are struck.

Surely I'm dumb and so beautiful in my outdoor face.

He will not be in any hurry,
said the oracle.

*

The oracle said:
You are the black horse.

I will numb
On hot flanks,
Sweat sweet
As heather.
My animal
Tang will
Be tender.
I will scrub
The midnight
Coat to a high
Gloss. I will
Bulldoze beds,
Install a track.
My garden,
Uprooted
For oats.
My kitchen,
Firebombed
For stables.

Unhurried,
everloved, you say:
if you're not interested...
and tease the threshold with your
jockey's foot.

You saunter, cap tipped low. Your hands were born to hold

       reins. There's gold braid on the haunches,
a whiskey shine on the saddle built for two.   I break

          into a canter. I tell the oracle. *I am afraid.*

                 I am allergic to the things that live.

All night, sleeping in the fireplace, the only four walls left, I croon
     lullabies an animal can remember:

   Soon, soon, leathercracker.   *Swoon, swoon, neckbreaker.*

I listen for the sound of chewing.   All night, I bless and bless my hives.

DEAR BLUEBEARD, DEAR LOVE

For so long I've been held here
behind the curtains of your body,

keeping my lusts and odors
to myself. I rust inside you,

rubbed past gristle. Past want.
Always such a perfect fit. Clickclick

go the doors. It gets
lonesome sometimes; my flesh

petrifies, wandering
these long halls. I call out to

turn the shadows strange.
Only the heads keep me

company. My girls. A sweet-tongued
army of three.

We commiserate—why do men
have to work such long hours, etc.?

I powder those still peach cheeks,
braid their excess of hair,

because it keeps growing, after,
and the nails too, bruise-hued spirals.

A busy man should keep things organized.
The faces whisper everything to me.

I line them up, all in a row,
brilliantly still and labeled, too, in case

you forget. The key makes a workman's
blade to extract what I like. MaryJo's

shapely nostril, the exuberant sponge
of Karen's right hip. Superimposed,

I'm so much more than a sum
of their parts. A pastiche in hourglass,

but my time won't run out. I swab them
too (between the thighs—I've no aversions).

It's rightfully mine, your residue
and the plumpest blue-eyed babies.

But at night, prostrate in your cold
sheets, that slug of envy. Why *them?*

Lissome, yes, but straight-laced.
Debutantes in fragile cornsilk.

Their words are fixed.
They could never love you like I do.

POSTCARD

In the kitchen, unblinking
tureen of borscht. The rosette
of radishes breaks my heart.
I drape boas on my throat,
practice accents.
The minutes stitch
to my little shames.
Dear sisters, I've forged
your names on another lease.
I've taken the top floor,
the shared bath, the governess,
her dropped sex,
the lessons in the basement.
I've sussed the beautiful animal
beards of men, the limitless
pirouettes of women.
Dear sisters, where are the periscopes
you've outgrown?

AFTER THE RECEIVING LINE

You can't say you don't enjoy it,
those seconds playing red

bird on the wire, sneaking the last
toffee almond from the bowl, chain smoking

in the church basement.
Your life so many broken zippers

& weather reports, darning
bridesmaid dresses of turquoise.

Your pearly whites are a buoy
to keep you afloat.

Your best friend's hitched;
you weep & tally mustaches

on your vanity. You can't keep her.
At the banquet, you perform

mating dances with the crab legs.
No one laughs

at peeling flower wallpaper,
the feet hostage in nude stockings,

bad behavior at the high-stakes dinner.
You slug apple schnapps & plan

the deaths of grooms by frosting,
imagine little black spats in sugary quicksand.

Are you a criminal, hardened
by AquaNet, or did you just mess up

the steps of the Electric Slide,
fill your dance card with pseudonyms?

You stand outside the ballroom,
crying your eyes out.

It's dawn. Your heel—
broken. She's delighted to be

finally getting away.
Men holler your name

out of trucks emblazoned PURITY MILK
Their white smocks contain multitudes.

They're hurrying as if their lives depended
on milk. They do. You've stood

at the center of this highway
for your whole life, thumb out, torn skirt,

steeling yourself for the slowdown,
ruing your pretty, arthritic bones.

DOLLHOUSE

Someone told me the password—EAT ME—
so I'm moving into the rooms one by one,
licking the dust off the tiny chandelier, tapping
discreetly on the ass of the skull-faced butler. See,
I've idealized this for so long, those curtains
of linen and lace, the exquisite eye-drop
wine cellar. I'd gladly lose a lash for that
diminutive footstool in port leather. Maybe
it's bigness that I'm after, a sense of perspective,
but I'm also learning how to talk with ceramic
madwomen in the attic. I hear they're looking
for a roommate. The façade is immaculate,
and the static on the dwarf television might be
the informal version of the prophecy. I'm rising
before dawn, chilly in my gross four-poster, so as
to sneak up on it, loom clumsy and enormous,
lunar. It's the first time my shadow has experienced
greatness since expulsion from my mother,
whom I suspect may be sifting through the garbage,
clipping the yellow roses. Maybe it's smallness
I want: my distinguishing features reduced
to the pricks of a pin. I'll wear my Jane Doll
nametag above the nipple, reduce my worldly
goods to a bundle at the end of a toothpick,
twist my petite tongue if they'll just let me in.

AUTOCRACY

It had been a difficult summer.
It had been a life without seductions.

Here, everyone composts the Sundays.
Everyone is entitled to a -35 second orgasm.

We leave our gentility for occasional rental.
There is work to be done, dust

on the busts of the stockbrokers.
All is cutting. All is edged with fuchsia

possibility. We bite into our shifts
like sworn carnivores. There is beauty,

even, in the absence of exits.
In the personal note (we rubbed spit

on the ink), you said: *Thanks for the bodies!*
Our moon nods, your moon winks.

SAY "PLEASE" BEFORE YOU TAKE MY HAND

I.

Gloves are back in fashion, as my ventures on Black Friday tell me. Ladies of fragrance display them on velveteen thrones. They are filled with plaster & loneliness. They whisper *take me, let me surround you, let me be your new skin. See, I come in all sizes & colors.*

The woman behind the glove counter brings her dog in. It's the ugliest thing I've ever seen. It doesn't pay to be selective with those that love unconditionally. She beams behind her tower of limbs. Over the store's Muzak, the squeals of discovery. We discuss the merits of various materials. Suede: "High maintenance." Rabbit-fur: "Warm, beautiful, cruel." Imitation leather: "Vulgar but ethical." Wool: "Built for endurance."

On Black Friday, women turn into banshees. A jewel-crusted stiletto arcs the store. I follow the rainbow. I pray there are no victims. When I dangle a handsome forest-green pair for inspection, the dog rears, seeking play, a tasty edible. *Get down on all fours, please,* the woman says, fighting her tears.

II.

Was he looking for a fit like a glove or a little extra income? I was looking for a chauffeur. Nothing particular in mind, long as he came buttoned and capped. Someone who knew when to raise the partition, to trap my phalanges in the glass, leave the fine ring of a bruise around the base of my fingers.

Traffic on the major highway slowed to a crawl. All around us, men shrugged off their black jackets and women slid their skinny ankles into the farrago. The sun bruised the sky. The concurrent flashing of emergency lights created a disco effect. His suit was too tight to dance in. Besides, a true professional will only do what's expected. After breakfast, I smoked cigarettes and swigged gin from a teacup of fine bone china. With a good man behind the wheel, you can afford to risk angina. I ashed his name onto the leather. My tongue loosened by the juniper,
I crooked my little pinky, whispered *Come hither.*

But where was the accident? The police vehicles, sleazy blue and white beasts in heat, wound around us. I detected burning, rapped sharply on the tinted glass. If we were going to be trapped for hours, I wanted the smell of him. If we were going to be trapped for hours, I wanted the detritus.

III.

Marriage is hard, says my mother, my occasional shopping partner. *Every morning, you wake up & it's there, that head on the pillow, waiting to hate you. When confronted with disorder,* says my mother, *put on some rubber gloves!* She's sage as ever. *Throw the whole mess into the machine, pour a cocktail, pull the lever.*

My mother and I circled the lot for hours, looking for the perfect place to park. She could be willful, crazed, indifferent to bulging fenders or the proper fit. But I liked gloves so tight they cut off the circulation. An elegant accessory can also prevent infections. But when he shook my hand, I wanted to feel the heat. To break the illusion of the skin's glove, and parse the circulatory system underneath.

IV.

Get down, he growled, *you don't want to see this.* The sky darkened with helicopters, mechanized vultures in pursuit of the meat. A single decision can make your life complete. Were the victims looking for trouble, a lovers' pact, or did they just lose control of the vehicle? My mother drove herself to the abortion, chickened out. The woman wrapped the gloves in fine tissue while the dog howled his defeat. Love is back in fashion. He found the biggest tip of his career under the passenger seat.

SPACE STILL AVAILABLE FOR THE MEMORY IMPAIRED

On my left the retirement home,
nyloned hobblers on the brutal green.
My knee is starting to give. *Piano legs,*
my mother said. *I'm a neck man, myself*
said he. I slow down to read the sign:
Space still available for the memory impaired.
My father lost it at fifty-nine, diapers
and an odor, calling me *Chink* over cheese
grits at the all-you-can-eat. Mile seven
& I intercept a line of fat-lipped girls.
Excuse us, ma'am, the blondest says, black
ribbons on her bicycle, & I'm twenty-nine
next week, but they're at that age of longlegged
nonchalance. *Nymphet,* my mother
called you, and my father hung around
too long when you came over, sectioned
oranges on a bright plate for *his princesses.*
I never told him how you said *your dad*
smells too sweet. Mile eight & I let myself
remember you won't speak to me
again. The rosebud blister on the big
toe. Your new language includes *toxicity*
& self-actualization, but I'm slow, all dumb
muscle & repressive limb-twitch. *Therapist*
rhymes with *ventriloquist.* Also *narcissist.*
The telephone's click is a breaking rib.
Mile nine & finally: the dull lung-thud
the body emits, the winning shriek,
my footfalls a Morse of *mercy mercy.*

III

CARTOON MARRIAGE

You and I befriended the birds, laughed
away the red eyes in the forest, the threat
of flesh and blood just beyond the house perimeter.
Our jolly songs! Our two dimensions! I cast you
as the pink-cheeked, hardy heroine, your stock
Norwegian-lite; I played the field mouse, the squirrel,
any foot soldier in the bevy of well-intentioned
rodents, cute and skittish. I was forever up
on my hind legs, eager to dust under your skirts.
Discarded storyboards littered our kitchen.
When the credits rolled, I finally sought
my hey-presto in your stadium-seat heart.
I cut with big-girl scissors, painstaking as a key grip,
and scooped it out, diligent, spirited. An animatrix
at the height of her powers, I'll live on that all winter.

SEMI-DOMESTICATED ARSONIST

I'm crazy about this trend in self-improvement.
Just say yes

to impromptu surgery, bigger garden gnomes,
the casual raze. Anyone looks better

with teeth marks removed from their cheeks,
an exposed exoskeleton.

Choose a few pounds in the right places.
I'm big as a house, and it's hard to hear

when a heart's at capacity. Scented candles
tempt me. The laundry won't stop running.

The mirror cuts off "no" to spite its face.
Wait: is this it, the site of your body,

those trick beams, deceptive paint job?
The real estate agent with the tidy bob said *Victorian,*

but Modern! Flames trellis the curtains.
With my spinster's salary, I can't afford the upkeep,

but I covet your eyelids anyway. Oh, the possibilities!
Those veined window shades, blue blockers of shadow.

Today I'll rip open the curtains,
seek directions for improvement:

nip/tuck, push/pull, yes/no, divide/conquer.
Does that mean assault & battery?

What I mean is: will you marry me?
I never claimed expertise with a scalpel,

or a blow-torch, but I've a way with a book
of matches. Don't look too hard (the fruit is real)

or worry—the emergency number is by the bed,
next to the rubber hose, the biohazard tuxedo.

RUSSIAN BATHS

The second most beautiful girl is the boldest.
She can duckfoot around the benches, untie the ribbons

of her hips. She is bold; she is silver; she cannot shame us.
The thistle under our arms. The dermal ruts, sulfur between our legs.

Our talk is bright, sparrowish. Kindergarten, that last trip to Mexico.
I've never seen sand so white. We face away from her,

salute the lockers. Grey steel, wheel of numbers. Not a mirror.
She unhooks her bra. She has all the time in the world.

There are many of us. The air is moist.
When we exit, we will beat each other, flank to shank,

with birch bound neat. We will breathe eucalyptus,
get a little high on chlorine. Yes, that is nice. You have a body;

it is my body. Acupuncturists say we shore our envy
in the spleen. We fit as tight as matryoshkas. We slit

our collective eyes, votives strung on the porch
of a late-summer party. We bathe her in distilled & terrible light.

Not an interrogation room. Not a flirt with red curtains.
There are women who come when called, who tell you what you need

without duress or torture. We all have something to sell
the high bidder. Our secrets, our Tupperware, our nasty lingerie.

At summer parties, our sweat is delicate & sweet
under our lace. We have dresses for dancing, for the egret chirps

of love, for cake. Fold chocolate into butter, frost twenty layers
and feed her. How much time we've wasted in another's life!

We hold her hair back, lovingly.
Lovingly, we clean the mess.

THE NEWLYWED'S GUIDE TO HUNTING

Do you remember what you killed,
the purple splay of it
across our windshield?
How we laughed at our luck,
disbelieving the body's splatter,
those crystals on rented glass.

Look at us, in our traveling clothes!
Your houndstooth cap, my rolling
suitcase. It's the sundries I can't keep
track of, the handcuffs, the skinner,
the extra shells, the matter
of the uneasy thud in the trunk.

I'm new to this and queasy.
Your eyes are blue as a sniper's lens;
your aim easy, your grip energetic.
I'm walking as fast as I can.
How did you miss my prosthetic?

Just drive, darling, and keep your eye
on the size of what's unsaid between us,
straddled and sweaty in the child's seat.
If you stay your big hands on the metal,
I'll control the timbre and the tempo,
confine my big talk to what's on the radio.
We'd be fools to stay, and we're fools

for acoustic guitar. On the Southern highway, we split
birds with the car. We don't know their names,
just so many burred, black hearts,
under the sickly stars. The blue of motel lights
paints over the center, that matte
blood on the dividers, guiding our way.

BIG GETAWAY FROM SMALL TOWN

It's all too fast, too much, and nothing ever gets really clean, but our valium's packed and we're ready for adventure! You tell me I look beautiful while screaming. I throw the crossbow superstitiously over my right shoulder and steady our clever decoys (wigged and festive) behind the porch screen. We hurry past these dilapidated factories, the lovely nights of heather. To not be or to be slated for departure. How I envy the teenagers, decorous with their half-smoked butts, yelling from the immolated church windows. They call each other bitch. You call for directions, or at least some goddamned answers. We've made a pie out of this fear and it might have won the local contest.

Will we miss the old mill, haunted with workers who return nightly to sort rough grain and inessential parts of automobiles? Our mechanisms are immaculate except for the freewheeling. I used to have this feeling that loneliness was no longer a possibility in the vastness of your arms, but now every word—charm, orgasm—is elided as CHASM. We used to burn fires in the basement of the mill so they'd resurrect, fill us in on the town's secrets. Would you love me more if I were the mayor's daughter? As midnight approaches, the leaping flames look more and more like a mouth. It's too warm to shiver. Maybe I can't cease being hungry because you're eating my liver.

We're young, broke and happy. Our suitcases have no wheels. We pass the time by stealing incidentals from each other: board game tokens, maps of the USSR. I want to bring my steel toe boots to the gas pedal and my ring finger to your lips. If we stay in town, the moon will sour on us and we'll go local, speak exclusively in ellipses. What's crouching amongst the machinery, the dullard cogs and levers? The mill men return every night to the site of the nickel and dime. The weeklies forecast an eclipse.

HONEYMOON IN LENINGRAD

I loved that phrase "to market,"
But the child didn't let me out of his sight.
He trailed, a grievous peacock.

He dragged my step like a tail.
I offered papaya, diamonds, klutzy origami.
Didn't my white breasts best the moon?

Why couldn't the birds fold up?
The play read: *cut him out in little stars.*
I pled with currency. Resinous charity,

I pledged. The child smiled. *You die lonely.*
The truth is, child, I die to please.
Eat, eat, I said. I was terrified of openings:

Mouths and loves and cavities.
I was always fifteen minutes late.
My true colors bled through the vacation album.

Oh rapture of the newborn, oh raptors of the grave!
Blame the palace bricks for my inscrutable bruises.
Oh glossy slop of czars. Nothing's perfect.

When the child started, he wouldn't stop
I knew nothing, except what I heard.
If you have questions, call the operator.

IF VERONIKA WINS THE PRISON PAGEANT

they'll cut her sentence by three months.
In the city today, they exhumed
Lenin for the fifth time;
Veronika's girlfriend taught her chess,
the pieces handmade from bread balls.
Veronika's long nails prick the faces in.
I sealed up all Veronika's love notes with spittle.
Before she left, we split our thumbs,
pressed them together like dead flowers.
Veronika's scar had the bigger smile.
Veronika writes: *Inside, a tube of Crest*
is worth 200 cigarettes.
Each time she stood me up
for the hoodlum down the road,
I learned another word for *traitor.*
Veronika complains about the meat, stringy tendons.
She's turning thin enough to escape her skin.
The potato's eye-sockets disapprove of her dye job.
For recreation, the prison girls chase lice.
Veronika misses the smell of small flowers,
the languor of the Black Sea.
If I want to comfort Veronika, I'll tell
her leisure is out of fashion in the city,
competitions all the rage; last I read,
Ms. HIV was crowned with a tiara of lilies
Every day she scrubs the latrines, reads
For a good time, call Gosha. I've had many
Goshas in my day—can't say
what sort of time. Veronika
can recite the famous games play by play.
Perhaps I kept my Queen too tight.

HUNGER

1.

Floss of your hair, cleave
     my tongue. New morning, new devil, do you make me

speechless or fluent as liquid? My words a dribble, hardening
     mid-air, but pleasure

freezes at the moment of its reckoning. Cleave my long thigh, grape heart;
     suture me from sleep with the anaphora

of your body, close, closer, closed.

2.

How your footprints had a different face. How the trees were scythes. How long-armed, how lace, how lovely. How the blueblack beetles & millipedes made love in our elbows. How far? How to decapitate a squirrel. How your boy-musk rose like a cape around me. How the word *hunger* sounds on the dry palate: your mouth, our earth. How sweet it is.

3.

Cat-eye moon on the night, will you shut
     the border, make a new sound for flesh? My fingers uneven

pyres to lend a glimmer—the stark pupil
     of desire at the center. I mime commands & picture you

downy at the copper-plated breast, stricken
     by your lullaby: *unrest, unrest, unrest.*

4.

When we lay in the canopy bed, you told me how lucky I was, because you are fastidious. *Faast.* I mouthed. *Id.* Other brothers, bad brothers, greedy, sucking,

hammer-toed, slate-hearted, would have eaten me, collapsed the plump kiwi of
my body into a digestive, gleaned the iron of my capillaries, the pearlescent marrow,
the tenderized meat of my brain. Instead, you counted my toes, glad there were ten.
You told me what happens to the hungry ones.

5.

Shoulder blades are slow as wind, but the stars seethe
        in uneasy plasma. Oh, copper-

hot armor, fall away, slow as an apple spiral, chasten
        the membranes of my lips. Tell me: are we not

out of the woods? Who can hear but the daft,
        dead birds, suicides on your windowsill?

6.

But I insisted you made me dream what I did. But you swam below that lid of con-
sciousness, and then the dream-sea was our mother and the cilia of lungs were the
blades of grass noosing our half-formed feet, and our heads fused like a vase of earth,
and our backs were one back, and our mother took the coil in her cold ringless fingers
and she wound it around & around & around us, and although I could not breathe,
I knew I would never be lost.

7.

All the horizon in handcuffs of color, and the morning
        rubs my red throat, dead wrists, but I cannot

mount your profile, or trick it to a mask; cannot
        harden enough to be the thing that lasts.

TAKE EVERYTHING FAST

There's no way to tell the women
from the men, thumbs equally lonesome
on the highway's shoulder. No way
to steep the pale music of the commune.
Our legs stick to the seats.
Our hands slough together like a dirge.
The mountains foam at the sky
& the flags of each protectorate whip the wind down.

We park in that quaint mill town,
with the Graveyard Preservation Society,
the single grocery stacked high with grey meat.
The clerk murmurs "paper or plastic?"
through a hole in the neck. We walk
the aisles for hours, dazed, all smiles.
Under neon, your face grows dearer.
The sons of mill men kill time at the drugstore.

We can pack Speedos, string bikinis, oxygen,
but the unmarked beach is quicksand.
We can't bring a picnic & forget utensils.
If there's noise, ignore it. And if disaster,
buy a manual. We finger our map,
affix our sticker. COEXIST, it reads.
We're nearly out of the woods.
The red leaves prove it, tangled,
brazen, in our hair.

THE CENTER FOR WRONG CHILDREN

You might ask, *wrong according to—?,* but all I do
is live with an employee, watch his white feet
at the end of the bed, and he claims there are plenty
of activities at the Center for Wrong Children. Duckhunting,
hammering nails. Ricky took fourteen
steelheads for his 2x4, called it toy, and brandished it,
cocky as all, Clark Gable, until he took out a face.

Aquariums and corn mazes. Waterslides and walks,
restraints and cops. There are snacks. They are full
of talk. My employee loses his appetite. My employee
is light as an egret. He's peering past, one leg sprung.
If I squint and squint, will his life appear? If I lie
on his chest, will he fly? So I slice the tallow off
the dinner candle, spoon ice cream, rue the moon.

A few lines ago, I wrote, *my employee is losing his life,*
purely by accident. *Accidents,* say the wise men,
happen. The supervisors at the Center are dedicated
to boundary-setting. If you sneak in after hours,
review the painterly arrangement of children
in their steel-barred windows. I'm locked up
on that word "wrong"—like done to, done?

There is no such thing as an accident, reads the selfhelp
book in the break room. *Happy Birthday!*
pleads the vanilla sheet cake in the play room.
Once a week, the parents give their fifteen
minutes on the horn. My employee's the type
to give the kids names like Carl Jung Money
and Big Jazz. I sleep; he sleepwalks. I kvetch

and he cries into his big hands. I fix a quip,
I fix my hair, I redecorate around him. I know
what you're thinking. Let's not pull the heartstrings,
OK? If you're anything like me, you
like to keep those fingers free of blisters.

I'm all: what can't be mended with champagne,
sex, a blazon of charades? The children make up
all manner of games. The other day, Sarah took out

Rhee's front tooth. There was "a lot" of blood.
They still don't know what came over her
fists. Some cultures might call this the hand
of God. Some call it inspiration. I pick change
from my employee's body when I'm bored,
swallow it. I've trained myself not to wince

at the metal. I've trained myself not think
about the toxins, the millions and millions of
occupying fingers. The term *condition* means
disease. *There's* sentiment *and* sentimental, a wise
man said. If I stay at it, maybe a money tree
will grow, and he can quit the Center. We'll
move back to a city, of strollers and scones,

a city of yoga and swans. At night, he's so thin
he gleams. He's so funny when he drinks. I just
can't take the smile off. Jenny has this thing about
touch. Jenny steals the stapler from the secretary,
scratches her forearms till they harden. She says:
my family tree. Some things should be said plain.
Like pain. Like sorry. The world is an evil place.

The caseworkers are up to their ears. They knock
around like atoms. They're trained to hear nothing
but the voices of children. *It's not personal,* they say.
My employee's all out of excuses. I'm all out of puns.
The Color of the Week is yellow. Fear, you see—
what do I know? The wise men said: *when times are dark,
what can you do but laugh?* I want to believe a word of it.

He wants a door as big as heaven. I want to break it down.
In the frame, the children are gargoyles, shouting their names.

DIPLOMACY

I weaved my confidence,
a wooden train,

through the covered tents,
the heavy canopies, talk's hard

spangle. The boys were proud,
in silk ties, comparing mock-ups

of their fathers. The grasshoppers,
the viscous violins!

The host, brash magnet,
diffused elusive kisses to the neck.

In one version, the beast
startles himself in the tall mirror

of the yawning hallway.
He pauses, pleased, to fix his hair.

In another version, the heroine
bites out stitches from her mother's corpse.

This was a time when real business
was conducted. A lock on the cellar, a note:

Unreliable! Please Do Not Attempt.
My mother stood still as an X-ray,

scrubbing invisible ink
from the water lilies on her apron.

The guests would not be thwarted.
This was the best part of the program.

AUTOBIOGRAPHY (IV)

You crooned: *you play tree, I'll play lightning.*

Funny!   ME TREE
YOU LIGHTNING.

You dreamed a house for me, at the edge of a desert.
It was my father's dream (Of course.)
It was my mother's terror.

      With clear views of an impossible ocean, cathedral ceilings,

And a single hallway reeling from light.

Only the lonely are holy. But what of the fact of the mail, the music
      of invitations dropped in a box?

Someone's fitting me into a cream dress.
Someone's bringing me cookbooks, and cold shrimp.

      You should be happy for me,

I say, bottom lip out. *I'm getting married.*
I slink past fear and into regrets only, please.

Why fear the lives of others? I ask the rocking chair, night after night.
The red umbrella of your smirk unfurled in my belly.

There was lightning at the party and a tiered cake.
O frail monolith of spun sugar, O grail
of all the grazing girls, puttering at the edge of the serene forest
dubbed coupling.

I stood in this cavern of women. I felt frail. I felt shaky.
"A person of nerves".
A person fickle as a candle.   When I finally crossed over

      into my real loyalty, your autocracy,

the women did their due diligence,
their lucent heads filling out

white caps, exclaiming—

Cue my: *I've just been so tired, so goddamned happy.*   I offer the sour
stock

of myself to them   and they ladle me up   and grow fat as panthers
                and they lubricate   and grow slick as panthers.

I curse you and swear to quit you,
                and you don't answer.

I bargain my dress and my parents and retirement account,
                and you don't answer
                                        You know the real enemy,

the women that ask so much of me, that signal *handle with care*
and sobriety
                with lips thin as swords and shellacked helmets of hair.

I am dry now, as the willow or the fir, whatever

                you prefer and I will implore you:

take me home and chop me up and make me forgettable as compost.

You say:
                you play garden, I play rake.

You, tuxedo jacket in the corner, jazzy, tricky-elbowed

riffing *arbor, ardor, flower, child*   over the mandolins.

You burned a hole inside   the meal inside me

                and called that dinner.

WOMEN AND CHILDREN FIRST

The day is beautiful, but all the fish are dead.
I'm waiting for the right moment to hate you,

but the deck is overflowing, & the music loud
and stinking as the sunflowers on the table.

As we board, we admire the passengers' getups.
It's all better done *al fresco*—even seasick babies

garbling hungers into the tiered skirts of the mothers.
Only the light of the Chinese lanterns makes me

misanthropic. Compass technology is out of date,
& anyway the captain's drunk on Skyy and saltwater.

I'm covering the first mate with quinine kisses
while you try out your phrenology with the Spanish

flamenco instructor. We make quite a pair, putting others
last, throwing them overboard. What's really past us?

What say you to decapitating the figurehead,
translating her long locks into kindling,

laying waste to her plaster belly, her guiding hips?
She'll give you a kiss before she goes out, spitting.

Our killing clothes are suspiciously
uniform: nautical stripes, high waists.

We accessorize with telescopes. Can't you see
I never had command, that I'm too distracted

with the feeding of the fish? I swear they're dead,
they're docile, sinking right into my empty hands.

I think that maybe you're the ship, so jolly
yet inscrutable with your sly eyes & big ribs,

which renders me the rudder or the shroud
& I prefer to be served—chilled champagne,

immaculate ceviche over a trio of cellos. We're tight
on low tides, saved by the thought of glaciers.

EMBASSY

The drawbridge has rusted again.
All hours of the evening, maids & guards
move, languid as chess, across the grounds
to place the stockade of stars, lance exotic
birds into the faults of the elms. Tonight's
shade of sky is "haze." Tonight's facts are
a tight dress. Invitations deposed like feathers.
Blue mold threads the display of cheese.
The closets are swept of local skeletons,
Alliances are the Great Danes, jaws shut
with import flowers. The grass of other countries
can blind the glare of any sky. We know now
we cannot return to the land of our origins.
Our hearts, those murky children, do not dispute
our boleros & bustiers. Even the river wears
a pink cape, the bodies of the salmon.
We know goodbye in six languages, hello in five.

ACKNOWLEDGMENTS

Grateful acknowledgment to publications in which versions of these poems appear: *Cimarron Review, The Concher, Country Dog Review, Fox Chase Review, Harpur Palate, Linebreak, Love Among the Ruins, Missouri Review, Witness, Prism Review, NOÖ Weekly, Sycamore Review, Tampa Review, Yemassee.*

Thank you to Bhanu Khapil for selecting the manuscript, and to Lisa Bowden and Kore Press for publishing it.

Thanks to Daniel Lin and LATR Editions.

While working on this book, I received invaluable support from the Sewanee Writers' Conference, the Vermont Studio Center, the Wesleyan Writers' Conference, Helen Zell and the University of Michigan M.F.A program, the University of Michigan Rackham School of Graduate Studies, and Pomfret School.

Thanks to the many friends, teachers, colleagues, and writers who have guided and inspired me: Andrea Beauchamp, Russell Brakefield, John Bacon, John Corrigan, Lisa Fay Coutley, Darcie Dennigan, Lucy Dinsmore, drunken boat, Laura Eve Engel, Aja Gabel, Linda Gregerson, Debora Greger, Ellee Hayes, Jeremy Heartberg, Chloe Honum, Marie Howe, Laura Kasischke, Kristin and Chris Karpinen, Kara Levy, The Lipp family, William Logan, William Lychak, Gary Lutz, Donna Masini, Khaled Mattawa, Raymond McDaniel, Klea McKenna, Pam Mulcahy, Eileen Pollack, Wallace Rowe, Danielle Sellers, Ravi Shankar, KC Trommer, Katrina Vandenberg, Adam Vines, Laura Wetherington, Carol Wightman, and Vita Zus.

Finally, thank you to my mother and father for love and encouragement.

Klea McKenna

Michelle Chan Brown's work has appeared or is forthcoming in *Cimarron Review, Linebreak, The Missouri Review, Quarterly West, Sycamore Review, Tampa Review, Witness,* and others. Her chapbook, "The Clever Decoys," is available from LATR Editions. She has received scholarships from the Sewanee Writers' Conference, the Vermont Studio Center, and the Wesleyan Writers' Conference. She earned her MFA at the University of Michigan and lives with her husband, the musician Paul Erik Lipp, in Washington, D.C. She works as Poetry Editor for *drunken boat.* See more here: **www.michellechanbrown.com**

standing by women's words since 1993

As a community of literary activists devoted to bringing forth a diversity of voices through works that meet the highest artistic standards, Kore Press publishes women's writing to deepen awareness and advance progressive social change.

Kore publishes the creative genius of women writers to maintain an equitable public discourse and to contribute to a more diverse, and accurate, historic record.

Why we publish women:
- Since its inception in 1923, *Time Magazine* has never had a female editor.
- Since 1948, the Pulitzer Prize for Fiction has gone to 42 men and 16 women.
- Of the 108 Nobel Prize Winners in Literature, 12 have been women. Three of the 12 female winners were in the last decade.

If you'd like to purchase a Kore Press book or make a tax-deductible contribution to the vital project of publishing contemporary women's literature, please go here: **korepress.org.**